D1577474

The Medieval Puzzle Collection

THIS IS A CARLTON BOOK

This edition published in 2014

by Carlton Books Limited

20 Mortimer Street

London W1T 3JW

Copyright © 2014 Carlton Books Limited

This book is sold subject to the condition that it shall not, by way of trade or otherwise, be lent, resold, hired out or otherwise circulated without the publisher's prior written consent in any form of cover or binding other than that which it is published and without a similar condition, including this condition, being imposed upon the subsequent purchaser.

Content previously published as *The Book of Medieval Puzzles*.

All rights reserved.

ISBN 978-1-78097-577-1

10 9 8 7 6 5 4 3 2 1

Printed in China

The Medieval Puzzle Collection

A FINE AND PERPLEXING TOME OF RIDDLES,
ENIGMAS AND CONUNDRUMS

TIM DEDOPULOS

CARLTON
BOOKS

Contents

INTRODUCTION **8**

SIMPLE PUZZLES Question Answer

The Courtyards 14 90

Barcelona 15 90

Wise Man's Bluff 16 91

Alcuin 17 91

Three Boatmen 18 92

Beam 19 92

Equity 20 92

Roll Out 21 93

Idiot 22 93

Riddle-Me-Ree 23 93

A Serious Meal 24 94

The Mason of Madrid 25 94

Smelly Water 26 95

Birthday Boy 27 95

A Bed of Roses 28 96

Looking Ahead 29 96

The Ox 30 97

The Bag 31 98

Illumination 32 99

5

	Question	**Answer**

	Question	**Answer**
In the Village	33	99
Magic Square	34	100
The Blacksmith	35	101
May and June	36	102
Firenze	37	103
The Templar Code	38	103
One Hump	39	104
Planking	40	105
Mine	41	106
Good Morning	42	107
Sour Milk	43	107
A Curious Design	44	108
Marek	45	108
Needle's Eye	46	109
Premium Brandy	47	109
The Count	48	110
Hundred Years	49	111
Cacciatore	50	112
Infamy, Infamy	51	113

MODERATE PUZZLES

	Question	Answer
Three Jailers	54	116
The Calipha's Garden	55	117
The Pigs	56	118
Three Squares	57	119
The Top of the Hill	58	120
Quite Contrary	59	120
Reales	60	121
Potato Farming	61	122
Black or White	62	123
The Mathematical Mason	63	124
Balance	64	125
The Ale Yard	65	125
In Norfolk	66	126
Bucket List	67	127
The Hunter's Spears	68	128
Ivan the Rather Unpleasant	69	128
The Battle Of Grunwald	70	129

	$\mathcal{Q}$uestion	$\mathcal{A}$nswer

Operators 71 130

Cassie 72 130

Monkey Puzzle 73 131

Always 74 131

Alhambra 75 132

Meissen 76 133

Old Tom 77 134

Scaling 78 134

The Heist 79 135

The Courier 80 136

The Moneylender 81 137

For the Cheese 82 138

The Heralds 83 139

Witchcraft 84 140

Saintly 85 141

Diptych 86 142

It's a Trap 87 143

Introduction

The world changes, time upon time. The Florentine way spreads amongst us all, bringing mighty upheavals, and everything that I have known seems certain to be shaken to the very core. Perhaps this is natural, and Man ever looks behind with longing and forward with dread. If that is so, then I am no different. The tides of fate are sweeping in, crushing everything, and when they recede again, I cannot say what they will leave behind. I suspect, however, that kittens will be involved.

So, it falls to me, in this time and place, to make a record of that which is vanishing. It is a gargantuan undertaking, and it would be hubris itself to attempt to chronicle everything that there is. My particular love is for games of the mind, for trials of wit and wisdom and insight, for stern tests of mathematical reasoning and the Aristotelian logic of the Organon. Thus I have restricted my efforts to this field.

In this tome, I have endeavoured to collect a broad range of interesting puzzles and other problems. Civilisation spreads far and wide in these times, yet only a fool would discount the clever nature of the seemingly barbarous peoples – strange to our eyes, alas – that cluster outside its wings. You never know where an intriguing puzzle may be found.

In exploring all possibilities, I feel that I have managed to assemble a pleasingly diverse selection of mental amusements. Some are arithmetical or geometrical, others matters of logic or insight. A few, indeed, are eminently practical. All of them have something to offer, I hope.

While on the topic of fondly optimistic anticipation, I feel I ought to at least acknowledge the possibility of this work surviving into posterity. Time is a ravening maw, in whose jaws we all are riven, mutilated and, inevitably, consumed. Its whimsies are utterly unfathomable. So, gentle reader, I cannot claim to know anything about you. Perhaps you are dear to me; or perhaps aeons have passed, and you have no form that I would even recognise as possessing awareness. The former seems far more likely. But, in case you are not able to ask me directly for elucidation, I have attempted to make each problem in this volume is clear as my poor, feeble mind allows. Likewise, the solutions to each problem are as detailed and penetrable as it is in me to permit. If there is doubt or error, then it originates with my own clumsiness, and I beg forgiveness.

There are many ways to catalogue a selection of things, as every collector and librarian knows only too well. For this volume, I have attempted to group problems by the approximate level of challenge that they offer – to my mind, at least. No two brains are the same, and that which one person finds blindingly obvious, another of equal mental capacity may find utterly obtuse. But I have only my own mind to go on, and arranging in this manner – rather than by location, say, or alphabetic order – allows for a juxtaposition of theme and challenge which I myself find pleasing. I hope it likewise offers you some pleasure.

As the world totters on the brink of irrevocable and utter change, I say this to you, my familiar stranger: take heart in the human spirit. Time is pressing, true – but never so short that a moment of pleasure is a waste. We have made it this far. We will endure, and the future... the future will be wondrous.

AUTHOR'S NOTE

In compiling this book, I have treated history in the same way that a magpie treats a jewellery box – I've grabbed names, places, and other shiny nuggets of random fact, and woven them into the nest of my puzzles. In other words, it's safest to assume that I'm taking horrible liberties with anything that looks like it might be real information. I'm sorry about that. However, I hope you enjoy the puzzles.

Tim Dedopulos, 2013

"The life so short,
the crafts so long to learn."

Geoffrey Chaucer

Simple Puzzles

The Courtyards

 LARGE HOME IN TOLEDO WAS BUILT SO as to consist of rooms around four courtyards, arranged as a square. Decorative gardens filled the space between. The buildings were constructed with an arrangement of numbers carved in place on the roofs, and inlaid into the statue at the heart of each courtyard.

What is the number in the fourth courtyard?

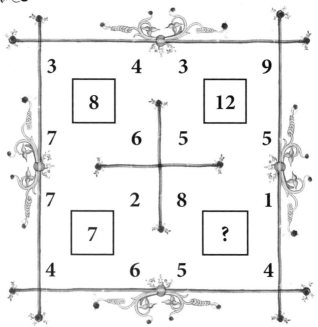

Solution on page 90

Barcelona

"**O**H, THIS WON'T DO! THIS WON'T DO AT ALL!"
The Seneschal to the Count of Barcelona was a
small, nervous man, and he was clearly flustered.

"**What is the matter?**" The Seneschal's assistant, well used to
his master's moods, managed to keep his voice patient, but he
could not inject any concern.

"The Count is having a small, personal dinner engagement
tonight. Everything must be perfect, and protocol is so variable!"

"Well, who is attending?" asked the assistant. "It cannot be
that troublesome."

"Oh my! The Count is expecting his father's brother-in-law,
his brother's father-in-law, his father-in-law's brother, and
his brother-in-law's father."

"So there will be five," said the assistant. "Even allowing for
niceties of status, that doesn't seem so stern."

"Oh, no, that is not at all correct," said the Seneschal, fanning
himself. "That would be fine! But that is the very most people
that it could be. The Count is expecting the very least!"

 The assistant peered at him suspiciously.
"How many is that?"

Solution on page 90

Wise Man's Bluff

ANCIENT LEGEND DICTATED THAT UNLESS the lord retained a certain number as advisers, the town would suffer disaster. Unfortunately, that number was clouded in vague language, and the Wise Men invariably disagreed with one another on every single topic under the sun. Simply greeting them with "Good morning" would lead to hours of impassioned argument. Asking them to agree on how many of their own number could be safely retired was utterly absurd.

The legend insisted that "The wise you must keep around you at all times. Without them, famine and pestilence will descend. They shall guard you by seeing all eventualities, in all manners of observation. Thus let there always be seven blind of both eyes, to see where sight cannot; two blind of one eye, to see in light and shadow; four with sight in both eyes, to clearly perceive danger; and nine that see with one eye, for the sake of clarity."

 What is the smallest number of Wise Men that will fulfil the requirements?

Solution on page 91

Alcuin

LCUIN, THE ABBOT OF MARMOUTIER ABBEY, was greatly fond of intellectual challenges, and had become known far and wide as a fierce scholar and teacher. One afternoon, he called his students into his office, and indicated to them five numbered sacks, which, he informed them, held grain.

"Pay attention," he said. "Each of these sacks contains a different amount of grain. Taken together, 1 and 2 weigh 12lbs. Similarly, 2 and 3 together weigh 13.5lbs. Numbers 3 and 4 weigh 11.5lbs. The last two sacks, 4 and 5, collectively weigh just 8lbs. Finally; it will be useful to know that sacks 1, 3 and 5 together weigh 16lbs.

What is the weight of each sack?"

Solution on page 91

Three Boatmen

HE MASTER OF A SMALL MARINA ON SAINT Mark's Basin in Venice found himself faced with a particularly trying problem. Some equipment had been stolen, and the witnesses all disagreed vehemently with each other. One of the men was telling the truth, but the boat master could not tell which one it was.

Stripped of all the hand-waving and flowery insults, the three boatmen's claims could be summarised as follows:

Arrigo: "Benci is lying."

Benci: "Cipolla is lying."

Cipolla: "The other two men are both lying."

 Which one should the boat master trust?

Solution on page 92

Beam

AN ARCHITECT, BUSILY ATTEMPTING TO BUILD a chapel, found that he needed to ensure that a beam was carefully balanced. If the alignment was off, the weight of the ceiling and arches would be improperly distributed, and disaster would undoubtedly ensue at some unfortunate point in the future.

This diagram summarises his problem – a beam of wood that has to bear two loads distributed unevenly from the point of balance. In this crude representation below, the marked divisions are all the same length. You can assume that the beam, rods and pivot point are rigid, and of negligible weight compared to the loads.

 If the left-hand load is fourteen hundredweight, what is the required right-hand load to keep the beam balanced?

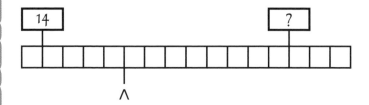

Solution on page 92

Equity

THE NUMBER 4 HAS FASCINATED theologians for centuries. Several Asian cultures consider the number 4 to be extremely unlucky, because their name for the number is very similar to their word for death.

It is a curious mathematical oddity that $2 + 2 = 2 \times 2 = 4$. Four is the only number that can be obtained by adding a number to itself and also by multiplying the same number by itself. However, there are many pairs of different numbers that can be both added and multiplied together to give the same answer.

 Can you find the pair that total 4.5?

Solution on page 92

Roll Out

ONE OF THE MOST IMPORTANT TASKS I'LL
have for you," the innkeeper told his new cellar-
boy, "is keeping track of how much ale and wine we
have." He waved at the row of tall oak barrels along the cellar
wall. "You need to be able to tell me when I get to half-way
down a barrel, so I can start preparing its replacement. I don't
want you using any filthy sticks in my beer, mind! You can
take the lid off and look, nothing more. Ah, don't look like
that, lad. Telling half-way is easy."

*So with no measuring device available other than
your eyes, and no indicators inside a barrel, how
would you work out when the barrel is half-empty?*

Solution on page 93

Idiot

THE VILLAGE OF WHITCHURCH WAS HOME to a particularly celebrated idiot. He was well known throughout the region for always having the wrong idea about money. You see, whenever he was offered his choice of two coins, he would inevitably take the lowest-value one, and then cavort off, utterly delighted with his erroneous choice.

One clergyman in particular had trouble understanding why the fool behaved the way he did. He tried an entire range of combinations on the man, testing coins of different sizes, ages and even shininess. Although the poor wretch seemed to have no idea of the meaning of value, he still somehow managed to always take the option that would leave him worse off. In the end, the clergyman was able to rule out the coins' weight, thickness, diameter, colour, lustre, and even age as the factor that made the idiot invariably descend on the offering of lesser value. It certainly wasn't just abysmally bad luck.

So how come the fool always took the less valuable coin?

Solution on page 93

Riddle-Me-Ree

NEVER SPEAKING, STILL AWAKE,
Pleasing most when most I speak,
The Delight of old and young,
Tho' I speak without a Tongue.
Nought but one Thing can confound me,
Many Voices joining round me;
Then I fret, and rave and gabble,
Like the Labourers of Babel.
I can bleat, or I can sing
Like the Warblers of the Spring.
Let the Love-sick Bard complain,
And I mourn the cruel Pain;
Let the happy Swain rejoice,
And I join my helping Voice.
Tho' a Lady, I am stout,
Drums and Trumpets bring me out;
Then I clash and roar, and rattle,
Join in all the Din of Battle.
Much I dread the Courtier's Fate,
When his Merit's out of Date,
For I hate a silent Breath,
And a Whisper is my Death.

Solution on page *93*

A Serious Meal

 ABBOT ALCUIN WAS A VERY FAIR-MINDED and mathematically careful man. When the time came to provide a meal to five labourers that he had engaged to build a wall, he was rigorous about ensuring that each man received exactly the same.

This was simple enough with most of the food, but the bread was something more of a trial. Three round loaves had to be divided between the five men. To keep everything equal, each one must receive identical pieces to the others. To help avoid boring the men, they were not to receive more than one piece of any given size.

Meeting these terms as simply as possible, what pieces of bread did the men receive?

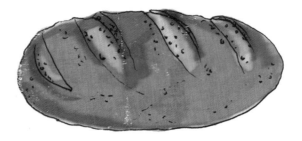

Solution on page 94

The Mason
of Madrid

N ENTERPRISING SPANISH MASON WITH AN
eye for the mathematical had a curious design carved
into the capstone of a well.

When asked about it, he would say only that it followed a
certain undeniable logic, and that he had left it incomplete
by way of a challenge.

 What is the missing glyph?

Solution on page 94

Smelly Water

A TANNER OF GIRONA WAS CONSIDERING A range of methods for reducing the amount of 'dung water' he needed to soak the skins. It occurred to him that he could use less if he wrapped his skins around a wide rod before dunking them into the rancid bath.

"So," he said to himself, "let us start with a cylinder to hold the fluid, where every foot of depth holds a gallon of fluid. Then there needs to be a rod, so assume that that every foot of that is equal in bulk to half a gallon of liquid. It will need to be light. Then, wrapped in furs up to the four-foot mark, it is lowered into the dung water. Hmm. Four feet of rod would displace two gallons of water, so the cylinder will need to be two feet higher. But wait, the rod will be taking up space there as well. So the rod will then displace another gallon of dung water. This will again rise higher, and then the rod will displace it again, and then... Merciful God! It will never end, and I will be drowned in the foul stuff!"

 Was he right to be worried?

Solution on page 95

Birthday Boy

MERCHANT WAS PASSING THROUGH THE village of Wedendorf on his way to Wismar, and decided to spend the night at the inn. He had been relaxing by the fire for a while when one of the locals came over to him.

"You look like a clever fellow," said the local. "Explain the matter of my friend Kurt's age – he's over there – and we'll each buy you an ale. Fail, and you buy us one. Do we have a deal?"

Amused, the merchant agreed.

"It's like this," the local said. "Two days ago, Kurt was 34. Next year, he'll be 37, and that is the Lord's own truth. How can that be?"

What is the answer?

Solution on page 95

A Bed of Roses

 GARDENER BOUGHT NINE ROSES TO commemorate the nine years he had been married to his wife. He also wanted to celebrate the eight children they had together, so he came up with a clever idea.

How would you plant them so as to end up with eight rows of roses, each row having exactly three flowers in it?

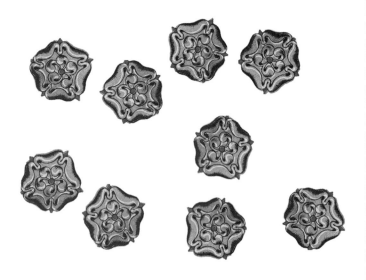

Solution on page 96

Looking Ahead

THREE MEN WERE SITTING ON SEPARATE tables in a market-side shisha house in Damascus.

They were the only patrons, for the working day was still on-going. Ibrahim was looking at Ahmed. Ahmed was looking at Sayeed. Sayeed, in his own turn, was carefully reading a bill of sale.

Now, Sayeed had hair of respectable length, carefully oiled and coiffured.

If I reveal to you that it was Ibrahim's proud habit to honestly describe himself as being as bald as an egg, is it possible for you to tell me whether, amongst the patrons of the shisha house, a bald man is looking at a non-bald man?

Solution on page 96

The Ox

LI KAO SETS OFF WHEN THE DAWN RISES TO drive his number ten ox to the local market. The poor beast is laden with many catties of rice, and it is not, by temperament, inclined to any great exertion even under the best of circumstances. Li Kao manages to goad the animal to an average speed of 900 bu per kè. His efforts pay off, as he manages to sell all of his rice in a timely manner.

On the return journey, with all burdens relieved, there is a pleasant breeze at their backs. The prospect of some well-earned food and rest enlivens both man and ox. Consequently, Li Kao persuades his ox to achieve the dizzying average speed of 1500bu per kè.

 In bu per kè, of course, what is the average speed for their journey?

Solution on page 97

The Bag

 JEWELLER AND A MERCHANT WERE discussing the nature of blind chance. They had some fundamental differences in their opinions, and the jeweller found himself getting increasingly impatient. Finally, he proposed a trial.

"I have two small silk bags. Into the first, I have put a round stone. I will tell you now that it is either a pearl or a cheap bead, one as likely as the other. I have also done the same with the second bag. The bags may both hold pearls, or both hold beads, or one of each. Now, I am going to put what is definitely a pearl – here, you see? – into the second bag, shake it, and then pull out... Ah, a pearl. So the second bag is back down to one stone.

 Now, my friend, without looking into either bag, is it possible to say which is more likely to contain a pearl?"

Solution on page 98

Illumination

MANUSCRIPT IN THE POSSESSION OF A particular Abbot deviated from the typical fare by delving into tutelary matters. It included the following curious diagram:

$$☉ - ☽ + ♃ = 7$$

$$☽ + ♃ \times ☉ = 50$$

$$♃ - ☉ + ☽ = 5$$

$$☽ \times ♃ + ☉ = 29$$

Assuming that calculations are performed in the order that they appear, what are the glyphs worth?

Solution on page 99

In the Village

OB AND BOB WERE STANDING BY THE WELL, waiting to get some water, when Bob spotted a tall fellow he didn't recognise.

Bob squinted at the man, trying to place him. "Here, Hob, who's the stranger over there? The bloke with the ratty beard. He looks a bit familiar."

Hob snorted. "He's not a stranger. His mother is my mother's mother-in-law."

Bob looked at Hob suspiciously. "Eh?"

 Who is the man?

Solution on page 99

Magic Square

ERMAN PHILOSOPHER HEINRICH CORNELIUS
Agrippa was one of the leading European mystics
of the 16th century. In 1531, he expanded one of his
previously published works to include the idea that various
magic squares could be associated with heavenly bodies. The
idea proved popular, and his squares, known as 'Kameas,' are
still a matter for discussion in modern times. In the square
shown part completed below, every row, column and diagonal
adds up to 65, and the numbers 1-25 appear once each. It is
the square that Agrippa associated with the planet Mars.

From the section provided, can you complete the square?

		7		
	25			
17	5	13	21	9
		1		
		19		

Solution on page 100

The Blacksmith

JOSÉ AWOKE ONE NIGHT TO THE UNMISTAKEABLE noise of someone fumbling around in his smithy. He was a big man, the tallest and strongest in Pedraza. People who didn't know better thought him slow, but the truth was that he was cautious with his movements, to avoid causing harm. Sometimes, his image emboldened thieves, who might have been wiser hunting elsewhere.

Leaping out of bed with a furious bellow, José charged towards his front door. When he got outside, he could see the intruder fleeing up the street. José set off after him. The thief was quick, taking nine steps for each five strides that José managed, and he had a dozen steps by way of a head start. But thanks to his size, three of José's strides were worth five and a half of the thief's steps.

 How far did José have to run to catch the thief?

Solution on page 101

May and June

MAY LIVED IN THE TOWN OF DERBY, WITH her sister June, and their mother. The sisters sold apples, and other fruits that became available from time to time. The pair was as identical as they were inseparable, which lent them certain fame around the town, and indeed they shared not only parents, but also the very hour of their birth. They dressed to increase the impact of their sameness, save that May always wore a red ribbon, and June a blue one – or at least, that was their claim, for there are times when an identical sister can be quite an advantage.

At least twice a day, some visitor to the town would see them and exclaim, as if it were a unique observation, "You must be twins!"

Their well-practised response was pitch-perfect, and utterly true. The two would look at the visitor, and in perfect synchrony arch an eyebrow and say, flatly, "We are most definitely not twins."

 Can you explain?

Solution on page 102

Firenze

 HERE IS A TREE THAT SITS AT THE CENTRE of a very particular courtyard. Next to it is a statue, seven feet tall including the pedestal, which commemorates a very particular person. At a specific time on a specific day of the year, the shadows of the tree and the statue touch very particular points on a very specific design carved into the flagstones of the courtyard.

At that moment... Hmm, perhaps I won't tell you what happens yet. Instead, I will tell you that the statue's shadow measures four feet in length, and the tree's shadow measures seven and a half feet, and maybe you will tell me the height of the tree?

Solution on page 103

The Templar Code

A FRENCH OFFICIAL APPREHENDED A suspected Templar sympathiser shortly after the Order's dissolution. He had a number of documents on his person, several relating to the chartering of cargo boats to transport unnamed items to Scotland. All of the important details were encoded. However, one particular pair of sums caused the official great consternation. They involved the consistent substitution of certain numbers with encrypted designs.

 One number was missing entirely. What was it?

		♄	♃	☉	×
			☉	♃	
=	♄	♂	☉	♅	♃	+
	♄	♂	♄	♅	♃	
=	2	4	6	9	6	
		♂	☽	♃	×
			?	?	
=	♄	Ψ	♀	☽	♄	+
	♄	♅	♃	♃	☉	
=	3	4	2	3	6	

Solution on page 103

One hump

PAIR OF CAMEL TRADERS WERE SWAPPING
shrewd observations on their relative ages during
a quiet moment. "Mohammed," said the first, "you
must surely realise that the numbers that make up your age
are the same as those that make up mine, merely reversed."
"Of course," said his companion. "Furthermore, the difference
between our ages is precisely one eleventh of their sum."

How old were the men?

Solution on page 104

Planking

RICHARD WAS WATCHING HIS GAFFER, Samuel, divide a plank into segments. Samuel sawed the plank exactly in half, clamped the two pieces together and sawed them both in half again, and then finally put all four bits in a pile and sawed them into eighths. Once he had dusted himself off, Samuel picked up one of the chunks and threw it to Richard.

"That was an 8-pound plank of oak, my lad," Samuel said.

Richard nodded. "Yep."

"So how much does that chunk weigh?"

"A pound," Richard said promptly.

Samuel snickered.

Why was Richard wrong?

Solution on page 105

Mine

 HERE IS SOMETHING PRECIOUS THAT you own.

You take it everywhere.
It weighs nothing but can carry weight.
You can share it with someone you haven't met.
Or even give it to someone you dislike.

Others may make more use of it than you do.

 What is it?

Solution on page 106

Good Morning

NE OF THE SMALLER COLLEGES OF
Bologna's famous university had a curious
tradition. Every morning, after prayers, each
student was required to bow to the headmaster, the tutors
and every other student. Similarly, the tutors were required
to bow to the headmaster, each other, and then the students
in turn. The headmaster, naturally enough, bowed to no one.

Over the course of the morning greetings, 1296 bows were
performed. Students outnumbered tutors eight to one.

How many tutors were there?

Solution on page 107

Sour Milk

ENA!"

"Oh. Sofie."

"You're not still cross about that milk, are you? You shouldn't have left it there. Look, are you going to the Rathaus this afternoon? I think the Bürgermeister is going to make an announcement about the taxes."

"I am going."

"When is it happening?"

"Hmm. Four hours before the meeting is as far past four in the morning as it is before four in the afternoon."

"... Ah."

 When is the meeting?

Solution on page 107

A Curious Design

 HIS GLYPH WAS FOUND ON A
long-forgotten stone in the centre of a dark forest.
The numbers surrounding it seem to suggest another.

 What number should be in the centre?

16

24   20

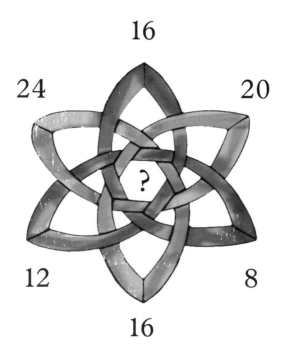

12   8

16

Solution on page 108

Marek

MAREK HAD TO TRAVEL TO KNIEJA, A TRIP of several hours. Because he was low on funds, the coachman agreed to allow him a reduced fare, the condition being that if his place in the carriage was needed, he would have to sit up on the running bench with the coachman, out in the cold, rainy weather.

At first, all seemed well, as there was just one other man travelling. But half way through their journey, they picked up several more passengers and Marek had to join the coachman. He stayed up there, shivering, until he had only half as far to go again to Knieja as the distance for which he had been out in the cold. At that point, a passenger disembarked, allowing Marek back into shelter.

 What proportion of the journey was Marek on the running bench for?

Solution on page 108

Needle's Eye

A MONK WAS IN THE TOWN OF ZARAGOZA, collecting charitable alms to help pay for the orphanage that his abbey provided. Having enjoyed some modest success, he came to the home of a minor member of the nobility, and despite some misgivings, decided to ask for a donation. The monk pled his case, and after some time, the lord's servant returned with a tattered scrap of filthy cloth, which he vehemently insisted the monk should take. He did so, and departed swiftly.

The following day, the Abbot sent a messenger back to the nobleman's house with sincere, enthusiastic declarations of his gratitude and appreciation.

 But why?

Solution on page 109

Premium Brandy

HE LANDLORD OF THE GREEN WITCH INN in Trewissick, Bill Hoover, purchased most of his spirits from free traders – smugglers, to you and me. Supply of brandy was always erratic, so he was in the habit of preparing a blend he sold to his customers as 'premium'. Making the blend was fairly straightforward.

First of all, Bill got two casks. He emptied a standard keg of brandy into the smaller cask, and fresh water into the larger. Then he tipped water into the smaller cask until he had doubled its contents. The next step was to pour the mix back into the larger cask until he had doubled that one's contents. Finally, he used the liquid in the larger cask to refill his original keg. You'd never have found such shoddy treatment at Mevagissey House, that's for sure.

How much brandy is in the old rogue's premium blend?

Solution on page 109

The Count

A MORAVIAN COUNT WAS WIDELY KNOWN to be in ill health, having had a weak constitution since his childhood. Eventually he ordered the construction of a resting room, where he might enjoy conditions as tolerable as possible. It was to be thickly carpeted, warmed by generous fireplaces on the other side of its internal walls, and well-lined with bookcases and paintings. So that the Count would have a view, he insisted that a square window be put in, five feet high.

Once the room was completed, all was to the Count's satisfaction – apart from the window. It let in too much light. The Count called the builder back, and demanded that the man alter the window to let in half as much light. However, he refused to allow the poor builder to change the type of glass, or add a curtain, or a shade, or shutters, or otherwise do anything to impact the quality of the viewing. In fact, he insisted that the window had to stay five feet high, five feet wide, and square.

 Eventually, the builder came up with a method. What was it?

Solution on page 110

hundred Years

ANY CURIOUS DESIGNS ARE TO BE FOUND in the caves of the Dordogne. Some of these stem from the times when the region was home to the long, painful struggle between the English and the French. There were moments when it was important to ensure that information remained obscure.

 What letters are missing from the third of these tablets?

3	8	5	2			
6	4	4	7	A	G	C
8	8	7	4			

5	9	0	1			
7	7	5	9	I	I	G
3	3	3	7			

7	3	9	6			
4	7	4	1	?	?	?
7	0	9	2			

Solution on page 111

Cacciatore

 HUNTER WAS SETTING A SNARE IN THE woods when he spotted a large hare across a clearing. He whistled sharply to his dog, and pointed to it. The hare took off, with the dog in immediate pursuit. The dog was faster, and immediately started closing the distance.

 The hare was 50 feet away when the chase started. If it took the dog 125 feet to catch the hare, how much further did the dog still have to run when there was just 30 feet between the two?

Solution on page 112

Infamy, Infamy

HE VILLAGE ELDERS GATHERED IN THE market square one evening to debate a knotty problem involving the behaviour of a young couple. One faction of the elders was scandalised, and felt that censure was the only option. The other faction was far less concerned, and wanted to leave the pair alone. Eventually, the unconcerned faction grew tired of the fuss, and wandered off.

It was noted in the alehouse across the way that if the woman who had called the meeting had decided to throw in with the unconcerned faction, then a full two thirds of the elders would have left. Alternatively, if she had been able to talk two of her regular cronies into staying with her, half of the meeting group would have still been there. As it was, neither of those things came to pass.

How many people attended the meeting?

Solution on page 113

"Wonder is the desire
for knowledge."

Thomas Aquinas

Moderate Puzzles

Three Jailers

HE MARIENBURG DUNGEONS WERE RIGHTLY feared. Enemies of the Teutonic Order found little comfort there, and the chances of escape were minimal. Part of the forbidding reputation came from the constant vigilance of the jailers, of course.

The task of watching one of the corridors was shared by three low-ranking guards: Matthias, Bernt and Konrad. At least one of the men was to be attentively on duty at all times, on pain of the most horrible punishments. But there were other restrictions to be obeyed. If Matthias was off duty, and Bernt was off duty, Konrad would be on duty. However, any time that Bernt was off duty, Konrad would also be off duty.

Could Matthias ever go off duty?

Solution on page 116

The Calipha's Garden

O SHOW HIS LOVE FOR HIS WIFE, THE Caliph of Baghdad decreed that a fabulous winding garden be constructed. It was almost square, just half a yard longer than it was wide, and divided entirely into the lanes of a single spiralling path. This mighty path, a yard wide throughout, was inlaid with semi-precious gems, and its edges were indicated with slender rods of copper. A great canopy of vines towered over everything, to provide shade. The path ended at the very heart of the garden, where a delicate fountain could be found.

 Including the space taken up by the fountain, the path was a majestic 7788 yards in length. What were the dimensions of the garden?

Solution on page 117

The Pigs

I T WAS TIME FOR THE LONG COMPTON PIG Fair. Farmers far and wide drove their prize pigs to gather around the King's Stone overlooking the village, so that the judges could evaluate their swine.

Old Hob had been judging the fair for years, and was thoroughly bored of pigs, so he decided to speed it up a little this year.

Pigs were graded on appearance, weight and height, and he had a number of performance tokens that he could hand out among the animals he picked as finalists for detailed grading. These tokens were classed either 'bad' or 'good'. The same tokens were used for each of the three things a pig could be graded on Hob decided to hand out 'bad' in at least one category to either 9 or 10 pigs, 'bad' in at least two categories to 4 or 5 pigs, and the wooden spoon of the finalists, three 'bad' tokens, to 2 or 3 pigs. Similarly, 8 or 9 pigs would get at least one 'good' token, 3 or 4 would get two 'good' tokens, and just one pig would be crowned the winner with three 'good' tokens.

Assuming that each finalist has to get at least one token, what's the least number of pigs that Hob can get away with giving tokens to, and what is the greatest number of tokens he can distribute among them?

Solution on page 118

Three Squares

N OLD MONASTERY ON THE FOOTHILLS
of the Hua Shan was reputed to be as ancient as
time itself. One of its most remarkable features
was an odd design, carved deep into the stone floor of a
small chamber, and set deep in the rock below the rest of
the monastery. It was said that to walk the design in one
continuous path, without ever treading the same line twice,
was to open oneself to enlightenment. Of course, no one
ever claimed that attaining enlightenment was easy.

Can you see a way?

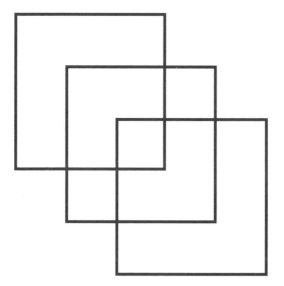

Solution on page 119

The Top of the hill

HE GRAND OLD DUKE OF YORK WAS SAID TO have ten thousand men. That is a respectable army, no doubt, but there have been many that have been considerably larger, both before and after. In France, a prince raised an army that consisted of 187 squadrons of cavalry and 207 battalions of infantry. Each squadron held four companies of 39 riders, and was commanded by a lieutenant colonel. Each battalion extended to three companies of 186 men, and was led by a colonel, assisted in turn by a lieutenant colonel.

Assuming that officers above the rank of colonel would rather not get their hands dirty, and that some 473 soldiers are presently incapacitated through illness, how many men can the prince send into battle?

Solution on page 120

Quite Contrary

**ALKING INTO A FLOWER GARDEN,
Lorenzo spotted a group of lovely young women
taking their morning ease. Wishing to make an
extravagant impression, he declared, "Upon my life! Ten pretty
maids, all in a row. Such beauty I did never hope to spy."**

The young women shared a glance. "Sir," said one of them, "your
eyes deceive. We are not actually in a row, and furthermore there
are not ten of us. However, if we were twice as many again as we
are, we should be as many above ten as we are presently under
that number."

"I see," said Lorenzo, and somewhat abashed, he took his leave.

 How many ladies were there?

Solution on page 120

Reales

WHEN ERNESTO MARRIED MARIA, HER dowry came in the form of her wedding gown. Her dress was strung with bandoliers of silver bells that tinkled beautifully as she walked.

There were four bandoliers in total, each one holding 27 bells. Although equally lovely, the bells were of differing sizes. Just less than a fifth were small, worth just 3 reales, and just under half that many were large, worth 8 reales. The remainder were of an in-between size, valued at 5 reales.

How much was Maria's dowry worth?

Solution on page 121

Potato Farming

ANS WAS HELPING HIS FATHER, KURT, PLANT potatoes. After a while, his father put the basket down and called Hans over.

"My son," Kurt said, "Tell me something. Imagine I were to ask you to bring a barrel of 100 potatoes to this spot. Then, I instruct you to take the potatoes out one at a time, and plant them a yard apart in a straight line, starting one yard from the barrel and leading away down the field. After each planting, you would come back to the barrel, and take another potato if one remained."

"My father," Hans said, "You can imagine I would tell you precisely what to do with your potatoes."

 Can you calculate how many yards Hans would have to walk to achieve such a thing?

Solution on page 122

Black or White

ON THE TABLE BEFORE YOU, THERE IS A BAG."

"Yes, I see it."

"Four counters are inside it. Each of the four may be either black or white, but they are otherwise identical. Without looking draw out two of them."

"Very well. A moment... They are both white."

"Excellent. What do you think the chance of drawing a third white counter to be?"

"Well..."

"Hold a moment. I meant to tell you that there was at least one white counter in the bag to start with."

"Ah! That makes all the difference!"

 Does it really?

Solution on page 123

The Mathematical Mason

 CERTAIN MADRILEÑO MASON DISCOVERED that an enigmatic well cover he had prepared had become the source of some speculation. Finding this fact to be rather amusing, he decided to do something similar with the lid of a large storage trough he was working on.

Can you complete the pattern?

Solution on page 124

Balance

HE PROCESS OF CONSTRUCTING A BUILDING is a delicate one. The proper balance of loads is vital. Without it, structures do not stay standing for very long.

In this crude representation below, a tricky issue of balance is reproduced as simply as possible. The marked divisions are all the same length. You can assume that the beam, rods and pivot point are rigid, and of negligible weight compared to the loads, which are given in hundredweight.

What value is required to balance the beam?

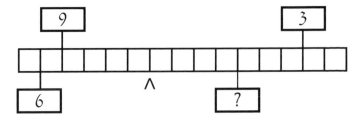

Solution on page 125

The Ale Yard

 HE GREEN WITCH INN IN TREWISSICK WAS known more for the cheap cost of its drinks than for their quality. They were certainly good value, which helped to offset the landlord's surly nature, and there was often less violence amongst the patrons than you might have found in other low-budget pubs.

The reason, of course, was that the landlord had a habit of watering down the ale. His standard practice was to fill a large jug from a ten-gallon keg, and fill the keg back up with water. Setting aside the pure ale for his own consumption, he would then fill the jug a second time with the weakened ale, which he sold at a slightly higher price, and again fill up the large keg with water. By the time he had done this, the mix in the keg was exactly 50% beer and 50% water.

What size was the jug?

Solution on page 125

66

In Norfolk

WORD QUICKLY SPREAD ROUND THE port town of King's Lynn. It turned out that Tom Mears, who had recently died, had in fact been married to the sister of his own widow! Folk shook their heads, and wagged their fingers, but the truth of it was inescapable.

 But how?

Solution on page 126

Bucket List

CARTER'S APPRENTICE, STRICKEN WITH curiosity one lunchtime, had part-filled a large bucket with water, and then floated a smaller bucket inside the larger. The water level rose, leaving the smaller bucket partly submerged.

As he was peering at it, the carter came past, and paused for a moment. "Do you see, lad? The floating bucket pushes aside enough water to equal its bulk." He wandered off again.

The apprentice looked at the buckets doubtfully. "But it's full of air. How can that be true?"

Solution on page 127

The hunter's Spears

 TAKE A LOOK AT THESE COLUMNS OF numbers. The left one adds to 19, and the right one adds to 20. It is possible, by moving one pair of numbers, to have both columns add to the same total.

How is it done?

1
2
7
9

3
4
5
8

Solution on page 128

Ivan the Rather Unpleasant

IVAN DOLOVICH FANCIED HIMSELF TO BE an important man. So what if the other merchants of Rovnoye did not agree? Having left a seemingly interminable meeting with some impertinent trappers, he found himself unsure of how much time had passed.

An uncouth fellow was passing, so Ivan Dolovich stepped into the man's path, and said, "I, Ivan Dolovich, need to be informed of the correct time."

The man, clearly not expecting such interaction, recoiled. Once he had regained his balance, he eyed Dolovich coolly. "I find your plight keenly distressing. Allow me to rectify such vicious injustice. Clearly, a masterful intellect such as yours will understand me precisely when I inform you that if you take a quarter of the current elapsed time since midday today, and a half of the time remaining between now and midday tomorrow, and add these two values together, you will have the correct time."

"Clearly," replied Dolovich weakly.

 What time is it?

Solution on page 128

The Battle Of Grunwald

HE BATTLE OF GRUNWALD WENT VERY badly for the Teutonic Knights. Poland and Lithuania combined forces to flatten them. Many men were lost that day, including the Grand Master himself, and although the Teutonic Knights survived as an order, their power never recovered.

Some time after the battle, when the Hospitaller of the Knights had divided the survivors into convenient groups, he sent his juniors to survey the injuries that the men had suffered. One of the reports was somewhat less thorough than he had hoped.

"Out of 100 men," said the lad, "64 have lost at least part of a limb, 62 are unable to grasp a weapon, 92 are unable to stand unaided, and 87 show signs of infection."

What is the minimum number of men unlucky enough to have all four problems?

Solution on page 129

Operators

 OBSERVE THE FOLLOWING SET OF NUMBERS:

$$1 \ 2 \ 3 \ 4 \ 5 \ 6 \ 7 \ 8 \ 9 = 100$$

This statement can be made mathematically accurate by placing just three simple numerical operators – that is, one or more of +, -, × and ÷. You cannot change the position of any of the digits, but you should treat any digits not separated by an operator as one number. In other words, 1+2 3 would be "1 + 23", while 1 2÷3 would be "12 ÷3."

 Can you solve the statement?

Solution on page 130

Cassie

CASSIE ALWAYS WORE PRACTICAL SHOES. They might not have been particularly lovely, but they were well-fitting and hard-wearing, and it would be fair to say that she hardly noticed them most of the time.

In fact, the truth is that she never took them off – not even to go to sleep at night – until she literally outgrew them. Even then, her next pair was always close to identical to the old ones. She truly wasn't obsessive about them, however.

 Can you explain?

Solution on page 130

444

Monkey Puzzle

GATHER CLOSE, MY FRIENDS, GATHER ROUND! I have a true marvel for you here. Yes, that's right, come up nice and close. Manel, the lovely lady monkey patiently clinging to the rope, has come to us all the way from far Takrur, and she is my invaluable assistant. My other equally invaluable assistant, Karim, is sitting over there. Oh, don't look like that, Karim. He doesn't like being reminded that he's as important as a monkey, my friends, but truly I am no more important than either of them.

The rope, as you can see, passes over a wheel and back down to a lump of genuine star-metal. It fell from the heavens, and when evil is near, it has been known to let out a chilling whine. And it is silent now! No evil here. But more importantly, it is the exact same weight as my beloved Manel. What you cannot see is the amazing cleverness inside my wheel, the finest in all Marrakesh, which allows the rope to move completely freely.

When I give the signal, Manel will start to climb the rope.

Cheer poor, sad Karim up by allowing him the privilege of taking your bets, and feel free to help yourself to a juicy date at the same time.

 Now, my friends, what will happen with the weight? Will Manel or the star-metal reach the top first?

Solution on page 131

Always

T IS A SIMPLE TRUTH THAT, THROUGHOUT
all of history, some things stay the same.
And so it is here.

In this sum, the numbers from 0 to 9 have been replaced
with letters, so that the same letter always represents the
same number.

 *If I tell you that none of the numbers shown begin
with a zero (0), can you tell me the final total?*

$$S \quad E \quad N \quad D \quad +$$

$$M \quad O \quad R \quad E$$

$$= \quad M \quad O \quad N \quad E \quad Y$$

Solution on page 131

Alhambra

 MERCHANT IN THE SIERRA NEVADAS NEEDED to make a delivery to the Alhambra. His route there took him along a flat road for a while, and then up a hill; his return journey took the same route. The actual delivery of his goods took just an instant.

On level ground, his pace was 4 miles per hour. Uphill, it dropped to 3 mph; downhill, it was 6 mph. He started his journey at 8am, and returned home at 2pm, before the worst of the day's heat.

 To within 30 minutes, at what time did he drop off his delivery?

Solution on page 132

Meissen

 THE MARGRAVE OF MEISSEN WANTED HIS sons to gain some fluency in numbers, so he had created for them a magnificent set of illustrated plaques, one for each of the numbers from 1 to 9. These he presented with a stern admonishment to care, and a challenge. Using all nine of the plaques, and nothing else, the task was to assemble four separate square numbers.

Could you do it?

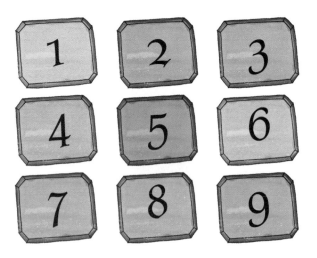

Solution on page 133

Old Tom

OW OLD ARE YOU REALLY, OLD TOM?"

"That would be telling, my dear. But maybe you can figure it out for yourself. In six years' time, I'll be one and a quarter times as old as I was four years ago."

 How old is Old Tom?

Solution on page 134

Scaling

 EVERY MERCHANT UNDERSTANDS THE importance of being able to measure the weight of an object. Weighing scales have been at the heart of mercantile endeavour for almost as long as human civilisation. How else is fairness to be obtained, other than through balance?

The diagram below represents several sets of weighing scales. Each of the scales is properly balanced, so that the weight of one side is equal to the weight of the other.

 Taking the smallest whole-unit values, what does each symbol weigh?

$$☉ ☾ = ☿$$

$$☾ ☾ ☉ = ♀$$

$$☿ ☿ ☿ = ♀ ☉ ☾ ☉$$

$$☿ ♀ = ☾ ☉ ☾ ☉ ☉ ☾$$

Solution on page 134

The heist

A GROUP OF ROUGH-AND-READY TYPES SPENT several long days in the taverns of Southampton's dock district, making plans. This included long periods watching one particular warehouse, owned by a respected wine merchant. After all their plotting was complete, the men waited until the small hours of the morning, then broke into the warehouse, overpowered the guard, and absconded with several hundred casks of extremely expensive spirits.

 The next morning however, the guard and the merchant were arrested, and the men were not. Why was that?

Solution on page 135

The Courier

WHILE TRAVELLING THE RURAL ROUTE from Briccolino to Cortanze, a young courier from Torino found himself with something of a problem. Not being familiar with the country, he relied upon the signposts along the way.

At one particularly complex five-way junction, he discovered that the signpost had fallen down, and he had no idea which road led onwards to Cortanze.

 What should he do to help himself find his way?

The Moneylender

A MONEYLENDER STOOD BEFORE THE KING, accused of being dishonest in his business transactions.

The King asked him:

"How much larger is four fourths than three fourths?"

"Why a fourth, your majesty." replied the moneylender.

A simple answer to a simple question. But the King banished the moneylender from his Kingdom.

 Why?

Solution on page 137

For the Cheese

FOR THE SAKE OF ARGUMENT, LET US SAY that Schoonhoven, known for its beer, is directly south of the hamlet of Mijdrecht. Gouda, rightly celebrated because of its creamy cheese, is about twelve miles to the west of the north-south line between Schoonhoven and Mijdrecht, and closer to Schoonhoven than it is to Mijdrecht.

Travelling from the latter to the former, you find that your route takes you via Gouda. Calculating only straight-line distances, the journey via Gouda is 35 miles in length.

 How far is it from Mijdrecht to Schoonhoven if you were to go directly?

Solution on page 138

 83

The heralds

SIR OSWALD RIDES OUT FROM YORK TO Lincoln, his horse travelling at a consistant eight miles per hour. Sir Edmund sets out from Lincoln on the road to York at exactly the same time; his steed travels at nine miles per hour but must stop every two hours for a five minute rest.

When the two knights meet, who will be closest to Lincoln, Sir Oswald or Sir Edmund?

Solution on page 139

Witchcraft

THIS ODD TABLET WAS FOUND IN THE HOME of a suspected witch in Seville. It breaks into four identically-shaped pieces, each containing precisely one of each of the six symbols.

Can you see how?

♌			♏		♂
			♏		
	♋		♋		♌
	♊		♊		♈
♊		♋	♋	♈	♈
♊	♈	♂		♏	♏
				♌	♌
		♂	♂		

Solution on page **140**

Saintly

A YOUNG LADY OF THE TOWN OF NYEN ON THE river Neva was the object of much attention within the town. This was partly due to her father's status as an Överstelöjtnant of Nyenskans fortress, and partly due to her loveliness and keen mind.

With most of the town's eligible bachelors to choose from, she was given to offering tests to would-be suitors. One such test involved the age of her eldest brother. She had fourteen siblings, born eighteen months apart on average.

The eldest, her aforementioned brother, was eight times the age of the youngest. How old was he?

Solution on page 141

Diptych

A FLEMISH PAINTER OF SOME RENOWN WAS IN the habit of encoding mysterious glyphs and tables within his masterpieces. This particular curious arrangement appeared in one of them, painted so as to appear carved into the wall of a cave.

 What value does each symbol have?

	27	26	28	25	
37	☉☿	☽☉	♀☿	♀♀	37
38	♀♀	♀☉	☽☿	☉☉	38
31	☉☽	☽♀	♀☉	♀☽	31
	27	26	28	25	

Solution on page 142

It's a Trap

A PAIR OF HORSE-PULLED TRAPS REGULARLY travels both ways along a particularly scenic section of the bank of the Vltava river in Praha. The journey takes a quarter of an hour, so the traps simultaneously depart in each direction every fifteen minutes.

A man walking the same route starts off on foot at the same time as a trap does. Twelve and a half minutes later, he meets one coming the other way.

 How much longer will it be before he is overtaken by that trap on its journey back out?

Solution on page 143

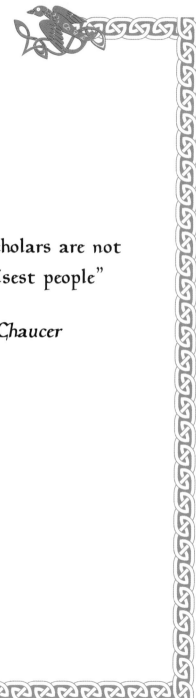

"The greatest scholars are not
usually the wisest people"

Geoffrey Chaucer

Simple Solutions

The Courtyards

8+1+5-4 = 10.

Barcelona

Just one man. The family tree is knotty, and assumes marriage between cousins is not forbidden, but it is possible.

Wise Man's Bluff

16 Wise Men in total. According to the prophecy, you need seven who are blind, and nine that see with one eye. But there is no requirement that one eye precludes the other, so the two who are blind in one eye and the four that see with both eyes can both be included among that initial nine.

Alcuin

The sacks weigh 5.5 lbs, 6.5 lbs, 7 lbs, 4.5 lbs and 3.5 lbs respectively. Considered together, each of the sacks is weighed twice, except '3', which is weighed three times. Add all the totals together, and subtract twice the weight of '1' and '2' combined, and also twice the weight of '4' and '5' combined, and you'll get 21, which is three times the weight of '3'. From there, you can substitute easily to find the values.

Three Boatmen

If just one man is telling the truth and the other two are lying, Cipolla has to be the honest man.

Beam

The unknown load is twice as far from the balance point as the known one, so must be half its weight – 7 hundredweight.

Equity

$$3 + 1.5 = 3 \times 1.5 = 4.5$$

Roll Out

Tip the barrel on its side just until the liquid inside touches the rim, and then look in. If the bottom of the barrel is visible at all, then it is more than half empty. If any of the barrel's side is hidden, it is more than half full. If the liquid reaches the join exactly, then it is precisely at the half-way mark.

Idiot

The 'idiot' knew perfectly well that as soon as he took the more valuable coin, people would lose interest and stop giving him money!

Riddle-Me-Ree

An echo.

A Serious Meal

Each man was given three pieces, namely a third,
a fifth and a fifteenth of a loaf. Divide one loaf
into five chunks, and the other two into thirds
(for six thirds). Chop one of those thirds into
five smaller pieces. You then have five thirds,
five fifths and five fifteenths to give to the men.

The Mason
of Madrid

If you count the stars up and treat them as
four-digit numbers, you will see that they are
a mathematical sum: 2615 + 4527 = 7142.
So the missing glyph is:

Smelly Water

No. Since the amount that the fluid rises halves
each time, it will in fact never quite get past
twice its original displacement.

Birthday Boy

It is January 1st, and Kurt's birthday is New Year's
Eve. Two days ago, he was 34. Yesterday, he turned 35.
Today is a new year, at the end of which Kurt will be
36. Next year, he'll become 37.

A Bed of Roses

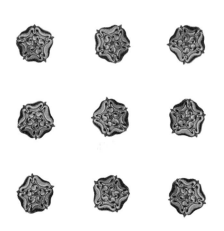

Looking Ahead

Yes (and yes). If Ahmed has hair, then Ibrahim is a bald man who is looking at him. If Ahmed is himself bald, then he is looking at Sayeed, who is not. Either way, there is a bald man looking at a man with hair.

The Ox

The answer is 1125bu per kè. You don't know how long the journey is, but it doesn't matter, since it is the same distance both ways. It is tempting to assume that the average overall speed will be exactly midway between the two speeds, but since you spend a longer time travelling at the lower speed, it gets dragged down slightly. Imagine, for example, that the distance is 4500 bu. Then it will take 5 kè to get there, and 3 to get back. Adding the speeds and averaging, we get ((3x1500)+(5x900))/8 = 9000/8 = 1125.

Now try it with a distance twice as far, which will take twice as long. ((6x1500)+(10x900))/16 = 18000/16 = 1125, again. The average remains the same.

The Bag

The second bag is more likely to hold a pearl.
The first bag has a flat 50% chance of holding a pearl
or a bead. The second bag has a 66.6% chance of
holding a pearl. When the known pearl goes in, we
know it holds two stones, either Pearl 1 (P1) and
Pearl 2 (P2), or the second pearl (B). That gives us
four possible ways that the jeweller could draw
two stones from it: P1 then P2; P2 then P1; P2
then B; or B then P2. We already know that he
didn't draw B first, so that last case is ruled out.
That leaves three possibilities, two of which
involve drawing a second pearl.

Illumination

$\odot = 5. \; \mathfrak{D} = 4. \; \math011 6.$

In the Village

The man is Hob's uncle.

Magic Square

11	24	**7**	20	3
4	12	**25**	8	16
17	**5**	**13**	**21**	**9**
10	18	**1**	14	22
23	6	**19**	2	15

The Blacksmith

It will take José 360 strides to catch the thief.
For each 15 of José's strides, the thief takes 9 x 3=27 of
his own steps. Those same 15 strides are worth 5.5 x 5
= 27.5 of the thief's steps. So each 15 of José's strides
closes the gap by half of a step. The gap is 12 steps, so it
will take 24 of these 15-stride periods – 24 ×15 = 360.

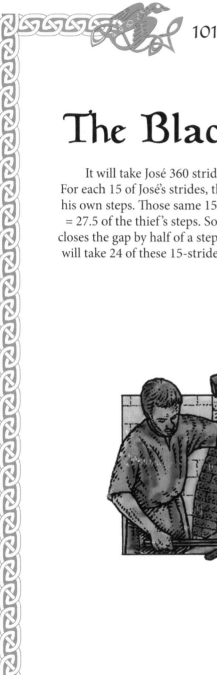

May and June

They had at least one more sister from the same birth – specifically, in this instance, April, the eldest of the three triplets, who lived in London.

Firenze

It is 13.125 feet tall. (7/4) gives the ratio of height to shadow, ×7.5 for the tree's shadow =13.125ft.

The Templar Code

The missing value is 75.
186 × 68 = 12648. 12648 + 12048 = 24696.
Similarly, 258 × 75 = 19350. 19350 + 14886 = 34236.

One hump

They are 45 and 54. The ages have to be close
together to keep the differential down to 1/11th
of the total, which implies a 9-year age gap,
and thus a total of 99 years.

Planking

Sawing wood consumes a certain amount of the raw material. After having sawn through the plank seven times in the process of dividing it, each section will now weigh a little less than a pound.

Mine

Your name.

Good Morning

4 tutors. People do not bow to themselves,
but the headmaster doesn't bow to anyone,
so 1296 bows means 36 people bowing.
One ninth of those are tutors.

Sour Milk

2pm. Midway between 4am and 4pm is 10am.
2pm is four hours after that.

A Curious Design

32. Opposing pairs of numbers are added
to make the number in the middle.

Marek

A third. He was outside from the halfway mark
to the point where he had half as far to go as he'd
already travelled out there – in other words,
if he had one part left to go, he would have been
outside for two parts. So he was outside for two
thirds of the second half of the trip.

Needle's Eye

The piece of cloth was a holy relic.
Possessing it would help raise the profile
of the abbey, and its income along with it.

Premium Brandy

Just 25%. He is diluting the brandy by 50%
in the first step, and then diluting that mix
by 50% again in the second step.

The Count

The window was rebuilt as a square diamond. That way it was able to stay five feet wide and high, and to remain square, but to only let in half as much light. In the original form, the window is 5x5 = 25 sq ft in area. As a diamond, 5ft is the length of the diagonal across the square. From Pythagoras' theorem, this means that the length of the diamond's sides is 3.535 feet, which gives an area of 12.5 sq ft.

hundred Years

BBI. Add the three four-digit numbers together on each table. Each of the last three digits of this sum – 173, 997 and 229 respectively – are then converted to letters that have that number's position in the alphabet. So 1 becomes A, 2 becomes B, and so on.

Cacciatore

75 feet. If the hare starts at 50ft distant and ends up at 0ft, then 30ft comes when there is still 3/5 of the chase left. 3/5 of 125 is 75.

Infamy, Infamy

18. The difference between ⅔ and ½ is ⅙.
The woman and her two regular friends make up
that difference. If 3 people are ⅙ of the group,
then the group is 3x6 = 18 people.

"Full wise is he that can
himselven knowe..."

Geoffrey Chaucer

Moderate Solutions

Three Jailers

Yes. If Bernt was on duty, Matthias could go off-duty.

The Calipha's Garden

88 x 88.5 yards. The length of the path in yards is equal to the area of the garden. Although the length and width are uneven, taking the square root of the area (88.249...) will give you an estimate of the value mid-way between them. You know the difference is 0.5 yards, so it is easy to check that 88 and 88.5 are the correct values.

The Pigs

10 pigs, receiving 29 tokens. All the different breakdowns can be stacked together, so two pigs received 3 'not so good', three pigs received 2 'not so good' and 1 'good' token, one pig receives 1 'not so good' and 1 'good' token, three pigs receive 1 'not so good' and 2 'good' tokens, and one pig receives 3 'good' tokens.

Three Squares

Try thinking of the design as several irregular pieces,
as below, and it becomes far more straightforward

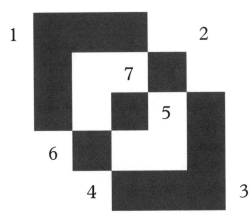

Start at the top left (1), and follow the outside edge
(2), (3) round to the bottom left (4). At the junction
immediately above (4), turn right and trace the inside
of the bottom right-angled section to (5), and then
come back down to the same junction (4) by tracing
the lower edge of the three little squares. Go round
to the next junction (6), and make the loop of the
edges of three little squares and the big right-angled
piece via (7). Finally, complete the loop by
coming back to (1).

The Top of the hill

144,806.
There are $187 \times (4 \times 39 + 1) = 29359$ cavalry,
$207 \times (3 \times 186 + 2) = 115920$.
$115920 + 29359 - 473 = 114806$.

Quite Contrary

5. Twice as many again would mean 3x their present
number, and for that to fall evenly either side of ten,
it has to be 5x3=15.

Reales

528 reales. 27×4=108. Just under a fifth
is 21 and just under half of that is 10.
So 21×3 + 10×8 + (108-31) ×5
= 63+80+385 = 528 reales – or 66 'Pieces of Eight'.
Not that Maria's father was a pirate...

Potato Farming

10100 yards. It would mean walking 1 yard there and back, then 2 yards, and so on. To quickly total 1 to 100, consider that it breaks down to 50 pairs of numbers each adding up to 101. $50 \times 101 = 5050$.
But the planter has to walk there and back, so it is twice as far.

Black or White

Yes; it increases the chance to $^7/_{12}$ from ½. The chance of drawing a third white out of a bag you know nothing about is 50%, as you would expect. If you know that there is at least one white counter in the bag, then there are only four possible initial states for the bag – (W)WWW, (W)WWB, (W)WBB or (W)BBB. The fifth option, BBBB, is impossible.

If we know nothing about the bag, we must assume the counters are selected randomly, which makes WWBB the most likely original state, and WBBB as likely as WWWW. When we know the fifth option is impossible however, (W)WWB and (W)WBB become equally likely original states, which pushes up the chance a little of drawing a third white counter.

The Mathematical Mason

If you count the stars and treat them as four-digit numbers, you will see that they are a mathematical sum: 4376 + 5007 = 9383. So the missing glyph is

Balance

11.25 hundredweight. On one side, you have 4×9 +
5×6 = 66. Take away 7×3 = 21 from that on the
other side, and you are left needing 45/4 = 11.25
to achieve balance.

The Ale Yard

In fact, the jug is 2.93 gallons in size. It has to be larger
than the 2.5 gallons one might expect in order to allow
for the fact that the second jug is no longer pure beer.
10-2.93=7.07 gallons of beer in the keg after one draft.
The next draft will hold only 70.7% percent beer, and
70.7% of 2.93 means the second drawing removes 2.07
gallons of beer. 2.93+2.07 is 5 gallons, for 50%.

In Norfolk

Mears was a widower. After his first wife died, he married her sister. His death left his second wife a widow, meaning that his first wife became his widow's sister.

Bucket List

The water that is displaced reflects the mass of the floating object. A certain percentage of the smaller bucket is still sticking up above the water, which adds to the mass. If the whole of the smaller bucket were suddenly transformed into as much water as required to provide the same weight, it would completely fill the space that the smaller bucket had occupied (up to the water line).

The hunter's Spears

Rotate the 9 and the 8 around their centre-point until they are in each other's spots, but the 9 is upside-down, and thus turned into a 6. Then both columns will add to 18.

Ivan the Rather Unpleasant

9.36pm. A quarter of 9h 36m is 2h 24m, and half the time to the next noon, 14h and 24m away, is 7h and 12m. 2h24+7h12=9h36.

The Battle Of Grunwald

Five. Total the number of injuries. The amount over 300 (representing the hundred men each having three injuries distributed amongst themselves) is the minimum number who have all four. 64+62+92+87=305.

Operators

123 - 46 - 67 + 89 = 100.

Cassie

Cassie is a horse.

Monkey Puzzle

Whatever the monkey does on the rope, the weight
will match her position. If she climbs up or down,
it will rise or fall with her. If she lets go and drops,
so will the weight. So they will reach the top at
the same time.

Always

The sum is 9567+1085=10652.

Alhambra

11:30 am. The route is the same both ways, so on the flat, a mile there and back takes ¼ + ¼ = half an hour. On the hill, a mile there and back takes ⅓ + ⅙ = again, half an hour. The journey takes 6 hours, so it is 12 miles there and 12 miles back. We cannot tell the delivery time precisely, but if the journey was all flat, 12 miles at 4mph would take three hours. If it was all hill, 12 miles at 3mph would take four hours. So 3.5 hours is definitely within half an hour of the delivery time. 8+3.5 = 11.5.

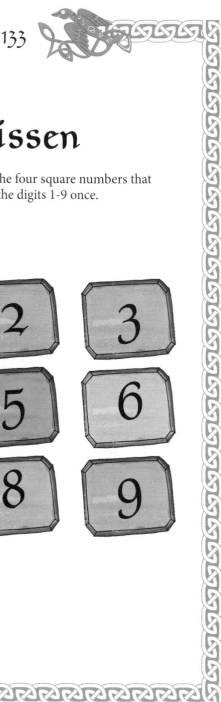

Meissen

9, 81, 324 and 576 are the four square numbers that together use the digits 1-9 once.

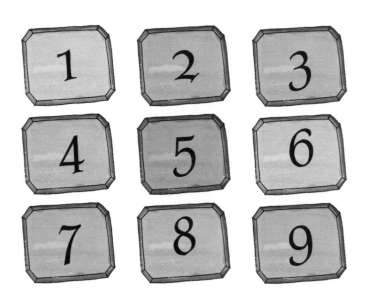

Old Tom

44. His age +6 is equal to 5/4th of (age - 4),
or 5×(age - 4) /4. Multiply out by 4 to get rid of
that divisor, and 4 × age + 24 = 5×(age - 4),
or 5 × age - 20. Add the 20 to both sides,
and 4 × age + 44 = 5 × age, or 44 = Old Tom's age.

Scaling

☉=1. ☽=3. ☿=4. ♃=7.

The heist

The men were enforcing the law, not behaving criminally. In this instance, they were revenue agents for the crown. The merchant was smuggling the spirits, and the agents raided his premises to confiscate the contraband and obtain proof of his perfidy.

The Courier

He should pick up the signpost and point it so that the sign to Briccolino is pointing the way that he had just come. Then all of the other indicators will also be pointing in the correct direction.

The Moneylender

A fourth is one third as as big as three fourths." with
"of three fourths. So four fourths is 1 and 1/3 the size
of three fourths – or one third larger.

For the Cheese

25 miles. Draw a horizontal line from Gouda to the North-South road and call the point where it intersects 'A'. Then we have two right-angled triangles, one Mijdrecht-Gouda-A, and the other Schoonhoven-Gouda-A. We know that the hypotenuses of these two triangles added together total 35, and that the length of Gouda-A is 12.   There are only three possible right-angled triangles with a side length of 12, and those have hypotenuses of 13, 15 and 20. 15 + 20 = 35. Those two triangles have sides of 9-12-15 and 16 -12 - 20, so the direct distance is 9 +16 = 25.

The heralds

This is a trick question of course. When
the two knights **meet**, they will be the
same distance from Lincoln.

Witchcraft

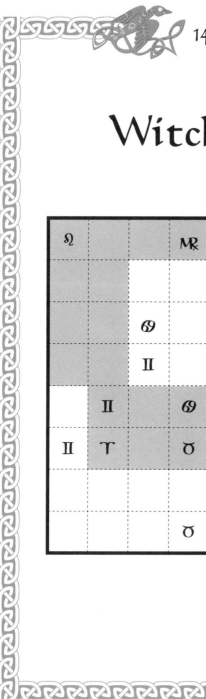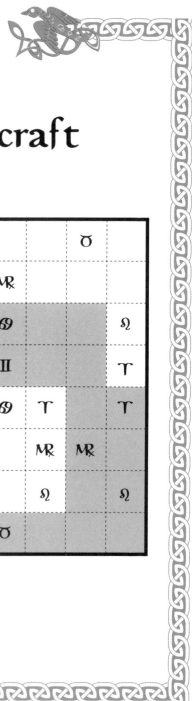

Saíntly

24.
Fifteen children means 14 age gaps, so 21 years.
The youngest is 3, the oldest is 24.

Diptych

☉=4. ☽=2. ☿=5. ♀=7.

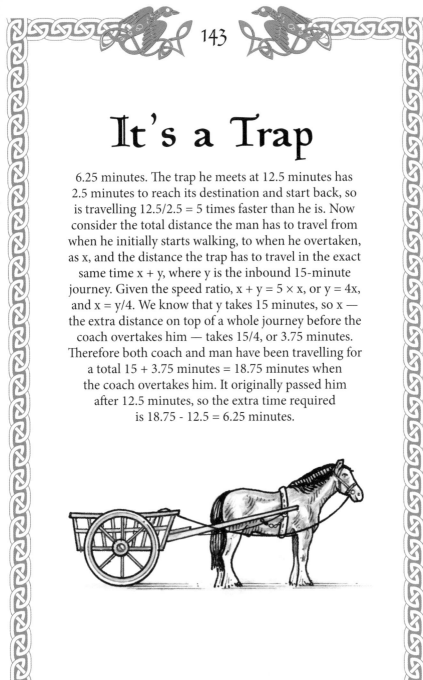

It's a Trap

6.25 minutes. The trap he meets at 12.5 minutes has 2.5 minutes to reach its destination and start back, so is travelling 12.5/2.5 = 5 times faster than he is. Now consider the total distance the man has to travel from when he initially starts walking, to when he overtaken, as x, and the distance the trap has to travel in the exact same time x + y, where y is the inbound 15-minute journey. Given the speed ratio, x + y = 5 × x, or y = 4x, and x = y/4. We know that y takes 15 minutes, so x — the extra distance on top of a whole journey before the coach overtakes him — takes 15/4, or 3.75 minutes. Therefore both coach and man have been travelling for a total 15 + 3.75 minutes = 18.75 minutes when the coach overtakes him. It originally passed him after 12.5 minutes, so the extra time required is 18.75 - 12.5 = 6.25 minutes.

If you enjoyed this book, you're sure to love *Sherlock Holmes' Elementary Puzzles,* also available from Carlton Books

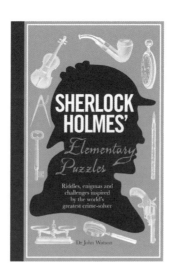

www.carltonbooks.co.uk